GROSS JOBS

Darla Duhaime

WITHDRAWN

Rourke
Educational Media

rourkeeducationalmedia

Scan for Related Titles and
Teacher Resources

TABLE OF CONTENTS

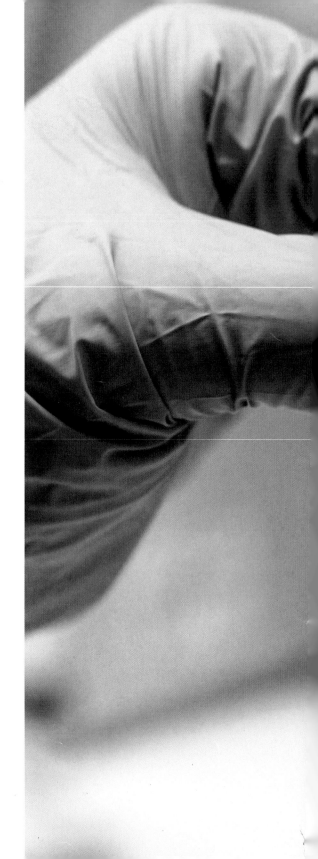

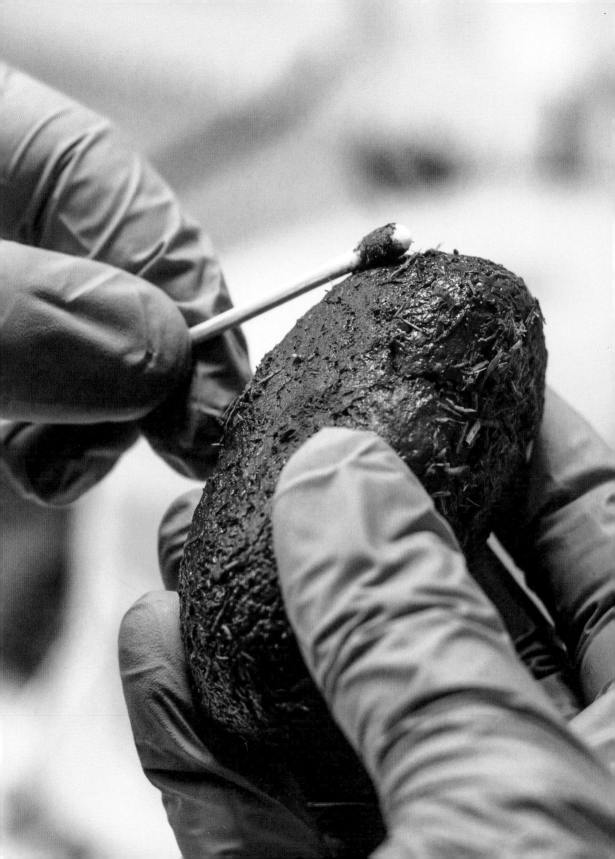

DIRTY WORK

Swimming through sewer sludge. Plucking insects off **corpses**. Sniffing other people's armpits. These are all real jobs. The work is dirty, but some of these gross occupations pay big money. Probably because most people would say:

GROSS ME

Maggot farming is serious business. And it's seriously smelly. The slimy, writhing fly larvae are raised for fishing bait and to supply greenhouses with **pollinating** flies.

The maggots are fed fish scraps. When they eat, they excrete **ammonia** to keep bacteria from eating their food. The smell is **acrid**! Maggot farmers say the stench is so bad, they must shower several times a day to keep the stench from settling on them.

Yuck!

A tray of 200,000 maggots eats about 275 pounds (124.74 kilograms) of fish in the week it takes them to become full-grown.

Deer are cute; we can all agree on that, right? But have you ever smelled deer urine? Talk about stinky! Deer pee is packed with **pheromones** that attract bucks. That makes it liquid gold to hunters.

Deer urine farmers collect and bottle deer urine for sale. Why would anyone want to be a pee collector? Because one deer can produce $93,000 to more than $300,000 worth of urine annually!

Urine isn't the only waste that can bring in the dough. Bat guano, or poop, is also big business. Bat guano collectors rise long before dawn each day to gather bat poo from caves. As they gather it from the ground, it's also raining down around them.

Bat guano is used as a **fertilizer.** Some farmers use guano for fruit trees because it's thought to make the fruit sweeter.

What do marine biologists want? Whale snot!
When do they want it? Now!

Whale snot is full of DNA, bacteria, viruses, and hormones that can tell scientists a lot about the creature's health and well-being.

Some researchers use drones to collect the gooey gunk they call "blow."

BODY

BAGGERS

You're in a car with the windows down—the wind in your hair, the scent of roadkill in your nose. Pee-yew! Ever wonder who cleans up when an animal dies on the road? The answer is roadkill collectors. These brave souls pick up carcasses and dispose of them in landfills or compost heaps.

Sadly, more than 1.5 million deer are struck by cars in the United States each year.

Mosquitoes, maggots, and flies are some of the insects forensic entomologists collect from crime scenes.

Crime doesn't pay, but gross crime scene jobs do. **Forensic** entomologists study the insects that **colonize** on dead bodies. These experts estimate the age of the insects feasting on a corpse.

This information provides clues about what caused the person's death and how long they've been dead. It can also provide clues about injuries, and indicate if the body was moved from one location to another.

After all the evidence is gathered from a crime scene, it's up to a special crew to clean it. Crime scene cleaners dispose of hazardous materials, blood, and guts. They may clean up drug labs and locations tainted with dangerous chemicals.

It's a gross job, but someone's gotta do it—and it pays about $600 an hour!

When a dead body is at a crime scene, the medical examiner will take the body back to the morgue for examination. The crime scene cleaners have to clean up and dispose of any remaining blood or visible signs of the tragedy.

When there's something nasty to dive into, HAZMAT (hazardous material) divers gear up and get dirty. These professionals swim through raw sewage, oil sludge, and contaminated waters to repair pipes, recover lost objects, or look for corpses.

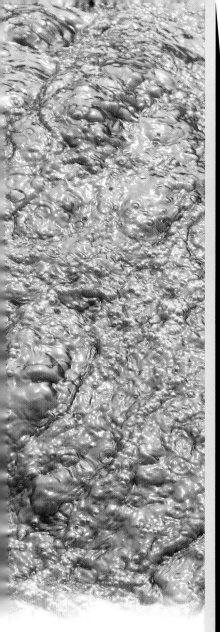

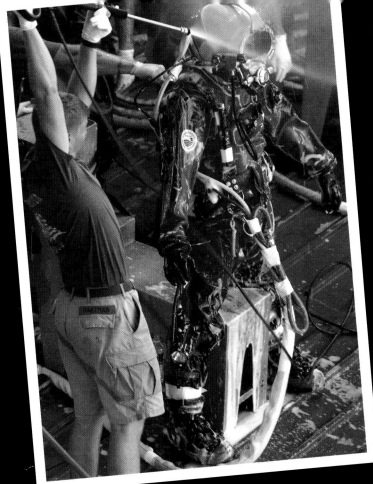

HAZMAT divers wear vulcanized rubber suits fitted with attached gloves and boots so no contaminants can enter. They also wear helmets, of course! They have to be decontaminated after each dive.

These dirty divers are vaccinated against many types of diseases, because they're constantly immersed in contaminated environments teeming with bacteria and toxins.

Would this be a good time to ask if you're hungry? Would you like some dog food? Animals can't tell us if they like a particular flavor better than another. That's where pet food tasters come in. These humans eat pet food for a living. Their job is to balance the tastes animals may like with the smells pet owners can tolerate.

Yum!

WHAT?

A pet food taster can make about $40,000 per year.

SCRATCH AND

Armpit sniffers work in a hot room, smelling more than 50 armpits an hour. They write reports on the effectiveness of the deodorant in controlling body odors.

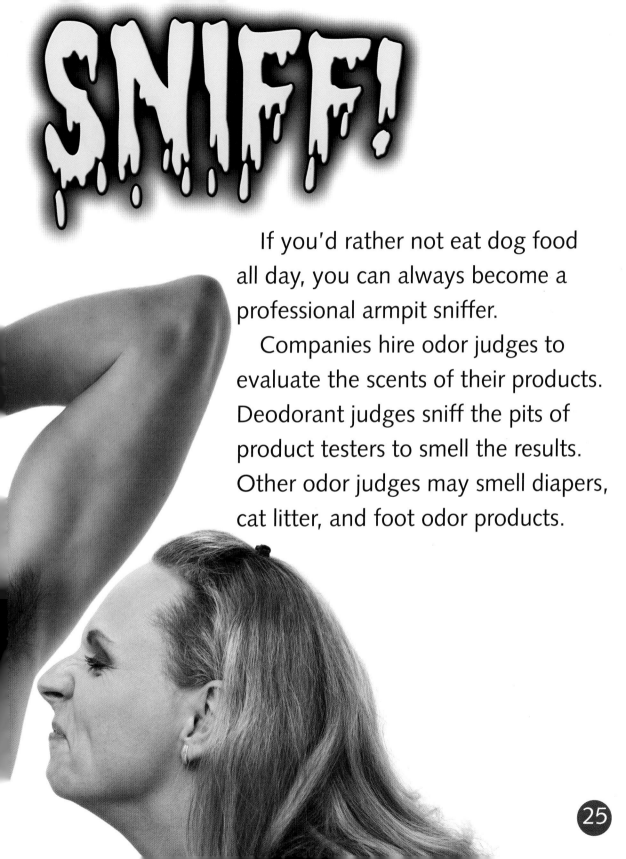

SNIFF!

If you'd rather not eat dog food all day, you can always become a professional armpit sniffer.

Companies hire odor judges to evaluate the scents of their products. Deodorant judges sniff the pits of product testers to smell the results. Other odor judges may smell diapers, cat litter, and foot odor products.

How does a mouthwash company test its products? With breath sniffers, of course! These odor judges sniff people with morning breath and after they've eaten strong foods, such as garlic.

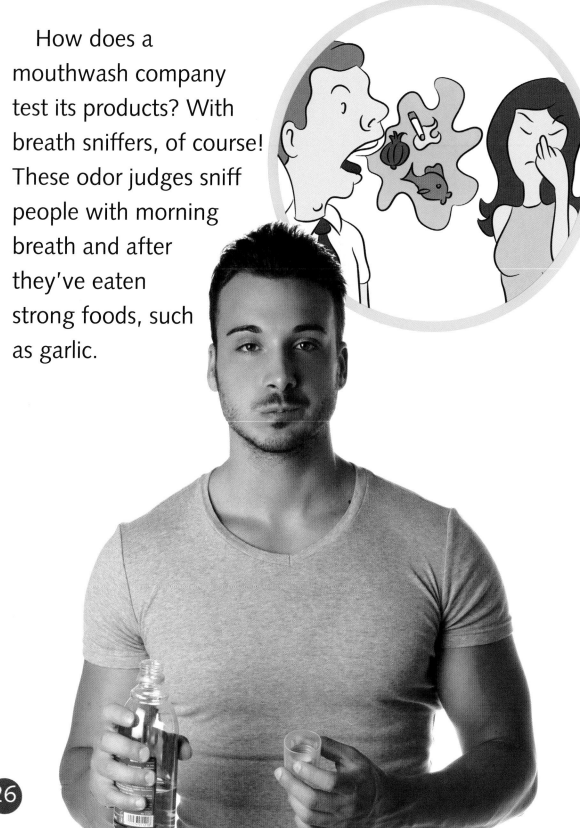

After the person uses the mouthwash, the odor judge takes another whiff and reports on the product's effectiveness.

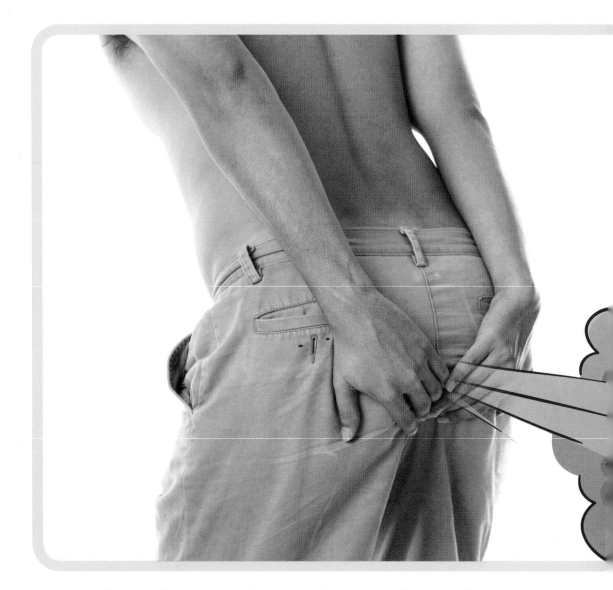

People with a nose for stink aren't limited to armpits and bad breath. Professional fart smellers are used by alternative medicine practitioners to diagnose health conditions.

Like dogs are trained to sniff drugs and dangerous chemicals, professional fart smellers are trained to recognize scents that are associated with disease.

A meaty smell, for instance, may indicate internal tumors or intestinal bleeding.

A certified fart smeller must be between the ages of 18 and 45 and have no nasal impairment. They also cannot use alcohol or tobacco. The job is reported to pay about $50,000 a year!

GLOSSARY

acrid (AK-rid): unpleasantly sharp, pungent, or bitter to the taste or smell

ammonia (uh-MOHN-yuh): a chemical with a strong smell

colonize (KAH-luh-nize): to establish a new colony in a place

corpses (korpses): dead bodies

fertilizer (FUR-tuhl-ize-ur): an organic or synthetic substance put into soil, so plants grow better

forensic (fuh-REN-sik): using science and technology to investigate evidence and establish facts to be used in a court of law

pheromones (FAIR-uh-mohns): a chemical substance produced and released into the environment by an animal, especially a mammal or an insect, affecting the behavior or physiology of others of its species

pollinating (PAH-luh-nayt-ing): carrying or transferring pollen from stamen to pistil of the same flower or another flower for fertilization

INDEX

SHOW WHAT YOU KNOW

1. Why is deer urine valuable?
2. What is bat guano used for?
3. What chemical do maggots produce?
4. What does HAZMAT stand for?
5. What does whale snot contain?

WEBSITES TO VISIT

https://kids.usa.gov/jobs/index.shtml

http://discoverykids.com

www.careeronestop.org

ABOUT THE AUTHOR

Darla Duhaime is a writer and purveyor of strange—and gross—facts from Sheffield, Vermont. When she's not writing, she enjoys picking wild berries, daydreaming, and cloud-watching. She likes to stay active and is known for keeping things interesting at family gatherings.

Meet The Author!
www.meetREMauthors.com

www.rourkeeducationalmedia.com

PHOTO CREDITS: Cover and page 17: Flies ©Paul venter https-_creativecommons.org_licenses_by-sa_3.0_deed.en.jpg, man © DWaschnig, woman (also on page 25) © Bacho; pages 2-3 © Fat Jackey; pages 4-5 GROSS ME OUT! letters © Cory Thoman, girl © Carlos Caetano, pages 6-7 maggots © Khing Pinta, page 7 © gasa; pages 8-9 deer illustration on bottle © CoffeeChocolates, bottle © Alter-ego, deer © Frank Fennema; pages 10-11 © sasimoto; pages 12-13 whale © oksana.perkins, green smear © timquo; page 14 © Valeniker, inset photo page 14 and page 15 The Blade, Rebekah Scott, 2001, page 16 © Roberto David; pages 18-19 crime scene © Photographee.eu, page 18 guy in hazmat suit © Gino Santa Maria; page 20-21 background © Noska Photo, page 20 diver © Savo Ilic, page 21 diver courtesy of U.S. Navy; page 23 girl © Eskymaks, dog food © Africa Studio; page 24 © Stefano Cavoretto; pages 26-27 illustration © John T Takai, woman with clipboard © Daxiao Productions, man with mouthwash © Stefano Cavoretto, stinky logo © SFerdon; pages 28-29 man © szefei, woman © pathdoc, fart graphic © Jeff Morin. All photos from Shutterstock.com except flies photo on cover and page 17, inset photos on page 14 and page 15, diver page 20 and page 21

Edited by: Keli Sipperley

Cover and Interior design by: Nicola Stratford   www.nicolastratford.com

Library of Congress PCN Data

Gross Jobs / Darla Duhaime
(Gross Me Out!)
 ISBN 978-1-68191-766-5 (hard cover)
 ISBN 978-1-68191-867-9 (soft cover)
 ISBN 978-1-68191-955-3 (e-Book)
Library of Congress Control Number: 2016932726

Rourke Educational Media
Printed in the United States of America, North Mankato, Minnesota

Also Available as: